ANTIPASTI

MADE EASY

ABIGAIL BROWN AND
MELISSA WEBB

NEW HOLLAND

First published in the UK in 2007 by
New Holland Publishers (UK) Ltd
London Cape Town Sydney Auckland

Garfield House, 86–88 Edgware Road
London W2 2EA
United Kingdom
www.newhollandpublishers.com

80 McKenzie Street
Cape Town 8001
South Africa

Unit 1, 66 Gibbes Street
Chatswood, NSW 2067
Australia

218 Lake Road
Northcote, Auckland
New Zealand

ISBN 978 1 84537 827 1

Senior Editor: Clare Sayer
Production: Hazel Kirkman
Design: www.bluegumdesigners.com
Photographer: Stuart West
Props stylist: Alison Murphy
Editorial Direction: Rosemary Wilkinson

Based on a design idea by Michele Gomes

1 3 5 7 9 10 8 6 4 2

Reproduction by Colourscan, Singapore
Printed and bound by Times Offset (M) Sdn Bhd, Malaysia

DEDICATION

MELISSA

To the hip chicks Lyla, Ana and Scarlet, along with the book
keeper and secretary.

ABI

To Pappa and Ma. Thanks for everything – past, present
and future.

ACKNOWLEDGEMENTS

We would like to thank Clare Sayer, our editor, for her enthusiasm
and patience; Rosemary Wilkinson for inviting us to do the book;
Stuart West for taking such beautiful photographs and Roger
Hammond for designing the book.

ANTIPASTI

MADE EASY

CONTENTS

INTRODUCTION

Think of Italy and you think of good food! Italian food is very varied and uses all kinds of cheeses, vegetables, meats and breads to create an array of tasty dishes. Bruschetta, soups, salads, cured meats, courgette (zucchini) flowers – this book includes all these dishes and the recipes are easy to follow.

We have both spent many summers in Italy from the Tuscan hills to the stunning Amalfi coast both on holiday and whilst working, cooking for clients, friends and family. The warm sun, beautiful scenery, fine wine and fresh produce makes it hard to resist a trip to Italy where the shops and markets are overflowing with wonderful food. We have both been inspired and have picked up all kinds of delicious recipes on our travels.

The word 'antipasto' means, literally, 'before the meal' and is the Italian version of a starter. Antipasti constitute the first course of usually four or five in an Italian meal, and are based on all kinds of dishes, including soups, salads, fried vegetables, meat and fish. Antipasti are very diverse, with lots of different dishes that will suit everyone, vegetarians and meat-eaters alike. They can be served in the Italian way, as a starter, or you can pick just one or two dishes to serve with drinks or, instead of a main course, cook a quantity of different antipasti for a long leisurely lunch with friends, with plenty of wine and conversation.

The good thing about serving antipasti is that you can just keep the dishes coming, in the manner of Spanish tapas, which means that the meal lasts longer, giving you more time to catch up with your friends and enjoy the atmosphere that you have created. Delicious food teamed with fine wine and company is the perfect combination for a great meal. The recipes in this book are both tempting and visually pleasing, too. Many contain fresh herbs so, as well as tasting good, they smell good too!

Cooking in Italy is a labour of love, and microwaves and oven-ready meals very rarely feature. Traditional Italian women would think nothing of spending all day in the kitchen preparing one meal; when their families gather together for a special occasion the day revolves around the meal, and these occasions can last all day, with many courses being cooked and eaten over many hours.

We hope we have managed to make things a bit simpler for you in this book, so you can cook and prepare your own introduction to an Italian banquet.

THE ITALIAN WAY

Gatherings with family and friends are at the heart of the Italian culture, and many celebrations, conversations and decisions are made over the dinner table. Most celebrations centre around a meal, with many courses being served unhurriedly over a period of many hours. Traditional family recipes are handed down from one generation to the next, with secret recipes kept within one family. Italians live to eat, and it shows in the wonderful food they produce. Every member of the family, from young to old, would be included in the preparation and enjoyment of a celebration feast.

Family meals are usually made up of five courses. Antipasti are the first, followed by the pasta, then the main course – usually meat with vegetables – then cheese, followed by something deliciously sweet. Naturally these courses would be served with plenty of fine Italian wines.

Italian cookery is based on rural traditions. You follow the seasons and eat only what is in season at the time. You won't find strawberries all year round or vegetables that are forced to grow out of season. Italians will wait for spring to eat fresh asparagus and for summer to enjoy ripe, juicy tomatoes and courgette (zucchini) flowers. This means that the dishes that are cooked are special to a particular time of year, and the ingredients used are full of flavour and colour. Italian tomatoes are the juiciest tomatoes you will find, with their sun-kissed flesh, rich red colour and delicious sweet flavour. From north to south the soil, climate and rainfall varies, so different regions are famous for different kinds of produce. Cattle are reared In the north so more butter, cheeses and meat are produced there. As you travel towards the south you will find more olives being grown so there are more olive oil producers.

Eating in Italy is a serious matter, and the Italians have created some of the world's most popular dishes, such as pizza and pasta.

Italian restaurants are popular all over the world, as they offer a varied selection of dishes that cater for all tastes. Italian food can be very simple, and employs the best fresh ingredients, olive oils, cheeses and meats to create interesting, flavoursome courses to enjoy. In most Italian kitchens you will generally find a bottle of olive oil or balsamic vinegar, some sun-dried tomatoes in the fridge and a lump of delicious Parmesan.

Convenience foods are very limited in Italy – you won't find an Italian mother using a jar of ready-made sauce for her spaghetti. Dishes are made from scratch and with great care and passion.

PRESENTATION

When you eat out in Italy, restaurants usually have a table laden with antipasti to which you help yourself. With the food being so varied in colour, shape, flavour and smell it is a wonderful experience for the senses!

Antipasti dishes are full of so many different colourful ingredients that they don't need much help to make them look good on the table. However, with a little bit of thought, you can make your food look stunning. We have mainly used white dishes in this book to show off the colours to best advantage but in Italy all kinds of different dishes would be used, including terracotta plates, wooden boards and baskets.

There is a huge range of kitchen shops, department stores and markets that sell all kinds of beautiful plates, bowls, soup cups and dipping bowls so experiment with different styles.

When you are laying out the food try not to overfill dishes and make them look crowded. Platters can always be topped up again as necessary. If pieces of bruschetta are too close together, for example, you will not be able to see the beautiful texture of the bread and fully appreciate the colours on the topping. Piles of food on plates can look rather cluttered and unappetising. When using raw or cured meats such as carpaccio, bresaola or Parma ham make sure you arrange them in a single layer only on the platter, then you will be able to see the texture and colour of the meat. And if you are drizzling olive oil or vinegar over them make sure all the pieces get a little!

You can use all different kinds of dishes for serving soup, from tall clear glasses for chilled soups, white espresso cups for little shots of soup, or square or round bowls for hot soups. Play around with different ideas and you will begin to find that your table looks really fun and interesting.

Garnish your antipasti with fresh herbs for an intoxicating aroma and additional flavour. Many supermarkets now sell pots of basil: buy two or three and put them on your table so your guests can pick their own fresh basil leaves straight from the plant. You can't get fresher than that!

EQUIPMENT

Working with the right tools helps to make cooking so much easier. You don't have to rush out and buy all the items suggested below but some things, such as a good sharp knife, really make the whole cooking experience much smoother.

Kitchen knives It's not necessary to rush out and buy a block of expensive knives, one for every job, but two or three good sharp knives will make chopping much easier. Generally we use three different knives: a small vegetable knife with a smooth blade, a small serrated knife and a large 20-cm (8-inch) chopping knife. It is important to keep your knives sharp and clean. Store them safely in a wallet or knife block. This keeps them out of harm's way and keeps the blades sharp. Of course, a sharpening steel is essential to keep the blades sharp. If you don't know how to use one or can't bear the noise, your local butcher may show you or even sharpen your knives for you!

Chopping boards In a proper catering kitchen we have to use plastic chopping boards for hygienic reasons but at home you can have plastic or wooden. We find the plastic boards easier to use because they are easier to keep clean and they do not retain the smell of garlic or onion. (There is nothing worse that cutting fruit on a board that tastes faintly of garlic!) If you do buy a plastic board choose one that is quite thick as the weight helps to hold it still when you are chopping (alternatively, you can put a tea towel under the board to hold it still). When you wash a plastic board make sure it is dried properly as it can smell if left damp. Of course wooden boards are still widely used – it is just a matter of preference.

Pots and pans Stainless steel heavy-based pans are the best to use. They are easy to clean and very durable. You can slowly build up a collection of different sizes as you get more into your cooking. A non-stick frying pan and small saucepan are always very useful. If using non-stick pans make sure you do not use metal utensils but heatproof plastic or wooden ones instead.

Baking sheets and trays It is useful to have two or three non-stick baking sheets and trays because they are more user-friendly. Do not use metal spatulas or utensils on non-stick trays.

Scales and measuring jugs It's important to have a good pair of scales, electronic or manual, and a measuring jug so that your recipes are accurate. Measuring spoons are also useful when it comes to small quantities.

Electric appliances None of these pieces of equipment are essential but they do make cooking much easier:
· An electric juicer for lemon or orange juice.
· A food processor is a fantastic piece of equipment for the kitchen, saving time when you are grating, mixing, chopping herbs and many other things.
· And last but by no means least, a good mixer is great for mixing, whipping cream, liquidizing and many other jobs.

Plastic spatulas The best thing to get all the mixture out of the mixing bowl without using your fingers. Now they are heat-proof and can be used in frying pans or woks.

Griddle pan This can be found in most kitchen shops and large department stores. A good griddle pan is great for cooking meat, griddling vegetables or lightly toasting bread for bruschetta. It gives food the distinctive line markings. A good pair of tongs is useful when using a griddle pan.

A few other utensils we find useful to have in the kitchen are: salad spinner, metal mixing bowl, citrus zester, kitchen scissors, plenty of wooden and metal spoons, baking parchment, foil and clingfilm.

INGREDIENTS

Shopping for ingredients in Italy is a real experience – everything is so fresh! In the markets the fruit and vegetables will probably have been picked that morning, or the day before, so they really will be ripe and ready to use. When you shop for antipasti ingredients try to buy really good-quality produce. The better the ingredients the better the end result. If you go to the market follow the Italian example and pick your own fruit and vegetables wherever possible, making sure they are ripe and not bruised. There are farmers' and organic markets to be found in many towns now so try to use them as much as you can. Organic produce does tend to be more expensive but the quality of meat and vegetables is better. Also, try to buy seasonal vegetables if possible so you get the best flavours.

There are some fantastic Italian delicatessens now that stock wonderful cured meats, cheeses and breads, so you don't always have to buy from the supermarkets. Explore the area where you live and try to find the best markets and shops from which to buy really good produce. Visit your local fishmonger for fresh fish, or a proper butcher for meat. Try to buy cheese from the cheese counter or a deli, and avoid pre-packed food as much as possible – you don't know how long it has been in the packet. If you shop in this way, fresh vegetables, cheeses, meats and so on will always taste better.

Once you get home from shopping, unpack the vegetables carefully and store them in the fridge (or dry store them) until you need them. Make sure that cheeses are wrapped carefully as some of then can be quite smelly and taint the other food in the fridge. Ten years ago people had never heard of sun-dried tomatoes but, like many other wonder Italian products, they are widely available almost everywhere, so you should have no problem finding what you need.

The following is a list of some essential antipasti ingredients:

TOMATOES Many antipasti dishes use tomatoes in all different forms – fresh, sun-blushed, sun-dried and roasted. The tomatoes that grow in Italy are so delicious, ripe and sweet they can just be sliced and served on their own with fresh basil and a drizzle of good olive oil.

PARMESAN CHEESE The most famous of all Italian cheeses, Parmesan – as its name suggests – is only made in an area near Parma. Parmigiano Reggiano is the best Parmesan to buy and has been aged for a minimum of two years. Parmesan can be eaten on its own with a good red wine or grated into hundreds of different Italian dishes to add delicious flavour. There is nothing better than freshly grated Parmesan on fresh pasta!

OLIVE OIL There are many different kinds of olive oil made in Italy and different regions produce their own, distinctively

flavoured olive oil. Extra-virgin olive oil is made by pressing the olives, with no further processing, leaving the oil with a rich fruity flavour and dark colour.

BALSAMIC VINEGAR A rich, sweet vinegar that can be used on its own, as a marinade or salad dressing. It comes from the Modena area and genuine balsamic vinegar has been aged in wooden barrels for many years, giving it its syrupy texture and rich dark colour.

MOZZARELLA CHEESE The best mozzarella you can buy is buffalo mozzarella, which is made in the area around Naples. The mozzarella is made using water buffalo milk and this makes a creamy, moist cheese with a delicious delicate flavour. Mozzarella can be used in salads just as it is or grilled (broiled) or cooked, as it melts beautifully.

BASIL This herb is an essential ingredient in Italian cooking. It has a wonderful aroma and very distinctive, intense flavour. Use it fresh with a simple mozzarella and tomato salad, to make fresh pesto or in cooked dishes. No Italian kitchen would be complete without a pot of basil on the windowsill.

OTHER USEFUL INGREDIENTS

STORE CUPBOARD

Pine nuts

Dried beans

Breadcrumbs

Black peppercorns

Tinned artichoke hearts

Tinned tuna

Tinned anchovies

Caraway seeds

Fennel seeds

Nutmeg

Truffle oil

KITCHEN SHELF

Onions

Rosemary plant

Fresh garlic

Parsley plant

Basil plant

FRIDGE

Dolcelatte cheese

Gorgonzola cheese

Butter

Olives

Lemons

Rocket (arugula)

Sun-blush tomatoes

Sun-dried tomatoes

FREEZER

Chicken livers

Small prawns or shrimps

Bread that can be defrosted
  and used for bruschetta or
  Panzanella

Chicken breasts

BREAD

PRAWN (SHRIMP) BRUSCHETTA WITH GARLIC CHIVES

makes 12

INGREDIENTS

12 slices ciabatta

olive oil for drizzling

salt and pepper

225 g (8 oz) cooked peeled prawns
(shrimp), lightly chopped

2 eggs

2 tbsp chopped garlic chives or
2 cloves garlic and 2 tbsp chopped
chives

2 tbsp chopped flat-leaf parsley

4 tbsp ($1/4$ cup) fresh breadcrumbs

grated rind and juice of 2 lemons

EQUIPMENT

oven tray

chopping board

knife

lemon zester

METHOD

Turn the grill (broiler) on to full.

Drizzle the ciabatta slices with oil and sprinkle over a little salt and pepper then place on the oven tray and grill (broil) on one side only. Set aside.

Mix all the remaining ingredients together, reserving half the lemon juice and rind, until you have a thick, gooey mixture that holds together.

Spread the mixture liberally on the untoasted side of the ciabatta slices and grill (broil) until golden brown.

Serve immediately with a squeeze of lemon juice and a sprinkling of grated lemon rind.

CHICKEN LIVER BRUSCHETTA makes 12 **INGREDIENTS** 300 g (10 oz) chicken livers, trimmed; 3 tbsp red wine vinegar; 12 slices ciabatta; olive oil; salt and pepper; 1 onion; 2 cloves garlic; 2 carrots; 1 celery stick; 100 ml (3½ fl oz) white wine; 2 egg yolks, beaten; 2 sprigs thyme, leaves only; juice of 1 lemon **METHOD** Soak the chicken livers in the red wine vinegar for 10 minutes. Prepare the ciabatta slices (see page 17). Finely chop the onion, carrots and celery and gently fry with the garlic for 5 minutes. Add the drained chicken livers and wine and season. After 5 minutes transfer to a food processor and give it three pulses. Transfer to a bowl and fold in the egg yolks, thyme and lemon juice. Spread onto the toasts, sprinkle with thyme and serve with lemon wedges.

MUSHROOM AND TRUFFLE BRUSCHETTA makes 12 **INGREDIENTS** 12 slices ciabatta; olive oil for drizzling; salt and pepper; 55 g (2 oz) butter; 3 cloves garlic, crushed; 450 g (1 lb) mixed mushrooms, e.g. shiitake, button, chestnut, field, girolle, thinly sliced; 3 black truffles, thinly sliced; grated rind and juice of 2 lemons; truffle oil **METHOD** Prepare the ciabatta slices (see page 17). Melt the butter over high heat, add the garlic and mushrooms, moving the mushrooms continuously. Season. When the mushrooms are slightly browned add the lemon juice. Divide the mixture between the toasts and place the truffles on top. Sprinkle over the grated lemon rind and drizzle a little truffle oil on top. Serve warm.

ROASTED GARLIC BRUSCHETTA makes 12 **INGREDIENTS** 4 whole bulbs garlic; extra-virgin olive oil; 1 bunch basil; 12 slices ciabatta; salt and pepper **METHOD** Pre-heat the oven to 150°C/300°F/Gas mark 2. Place each garlic bulb into a piece of foil and drizzle with oil. Bake for 30 minutes until soft. Prepare the ciabatta slices (see page 17). Take one third of each cooked garlic bulb and squeeze the cloves out of their skins. Squash the cloves with a fork in a bowl until you have a spreading mixture, taste and season. With the remaining garlic carefully take off the skins, trying to keep the cloves whole. Take the garlic paste and spread on the toasts, top with a basil leaf and then add the roasted whole cloves. Drizzle with oil, season and serve.

GRIDDLED ARTICHOKE HEART BRUSCHETTA makes 12 **INGREDIENTS** 12 slices ciabatta; extra-virgin olive oil; 2 cloves garlic, peeled and cut in half; 2 400-g (14-oz) jars baby artichoke hearts, drained and sliced in half; 1 small bunch flat-leaf parsley, roughly chopped; salt and pepper; juice of 1 lemon **METHOD** Place a griddle pan on the hob and heat. Prepare the ciabatta slices (see page 17). While still hot rub with the garlic. Place the artichokes on the griddle – you just want to give them the grilled (broiled) effect on both sides as they are already cooked. In a bowl mix the artichokes with the parsley, seasoning and lemon juice. Place on top of the toasts and serve.

MOZZARELLA AND ROASTED RED ONION CROSTINI

makes 12

INGREDIENTS

4 red onions, peeled and cut into
   wedges

olive oil for drizzling

2 tbsp caster (superfine) sugar

6 slices country bread

salt and pepper

225 g (8 oz) mozzarella, cut into
   bite-sized pieces

1 small bunch basil

EQUIPMENT

griddle pan

chopping board

knife

lemon zester

METHOD

Pre-heat the oven to 200°C/400°F/Gas mark 6.

Place the onions on a baking tray, drizzle with oil and sprinkle with the sugar. Cook until they become golden and soft. This will take about 30 minutes and can be done a day in advance.

Heat the griddle pan on the hob until smoking, drizzle the bread with oil and griddle the bread on both sides.

Slice the griddled bread in half, drizzle with oil and sprinkle over a little salt and pepper. Place the mozzarella and onions on the toasts, season, top with basil leaves and drizzle with oil.

MIXED BEAN CROSTINI makes 12 **INGREDIENTS** 150g (5 oz) dried mixed Tuscan beans (cannellini and borlotti); 6 slices country bread; olive oil for drizzling; salt and pepper; grated rind and juice of 1 lemon; 2 bunches wild rocket (arugula) **METHOD** Cover the beans with water in a large bowl and leave to soak overnight. Boil the beans in water for 10 minutes and then simmer for 40 minutes. Heat the griddle pan on the hob until smoking. Cut the bread slices in half and drizzle with oil, sprinkle over a little salt and pepper then griddle on both sides. Using a potato masher, squash the beans very slightly, season and add the lemon rind and juice. Lay the rocket (arugula) on the crostini, top with the bean mixture and drizzle with oil.

PRAWN (SHRIMP) AND VEGETABLE CROSTINI makes 12 **INGREDIENTS** 6 slices country bread; olive oil for drizzling; salt and pepper; 24 prawns (shrimp); 1 red and 1 yellow pepper, cut into chunks the size of the prawns (shrimp); 4 cloves garlic, thinly sliced; 2 courgettes (zucchini), cut into chunks the size of the prawns (shrimp) **METHOD** Heat the griddle pan on the hob until smoking. Cut the bread slices in half and drizzle with oil, sprinkle over a little salt and pepper then griddle on both sides. Heat a frying pan until very hot, drizzle in some oil in and add the prawns (shrimp). Sauté on both sides for a couple of minutes then set aside. Add the peppers, garlic and courgettes (zucchini) and a little more oil. Season. When they are tender and have a good colour on them add to the prawns (shrimp). Divide the mixture between the toasts and drizzle with oil.

SMOKED SALMON BUTTER CROSTINI makes 12 **INGREDIENTS** 6 slices country bread; olive oil for drizzling; salt and pepper; 100g (3$\frac{1}{2}$ oz) unsalted butter, softened; 100g (3$\frac{1}{2}$ oz) smoked salmon, diced; 2 lemons, sliced **METHOD** Heat the griddle pan on the hob until smoking. Cut the bread slices in half and drizzle with oil, sprinkle over a little salt and pepper then griddle on both sides. In a bowl fork through the butter and add the smoked salmon, season then add a squeeze of lemon. Place on the toasts and garnish with more ground pepper.

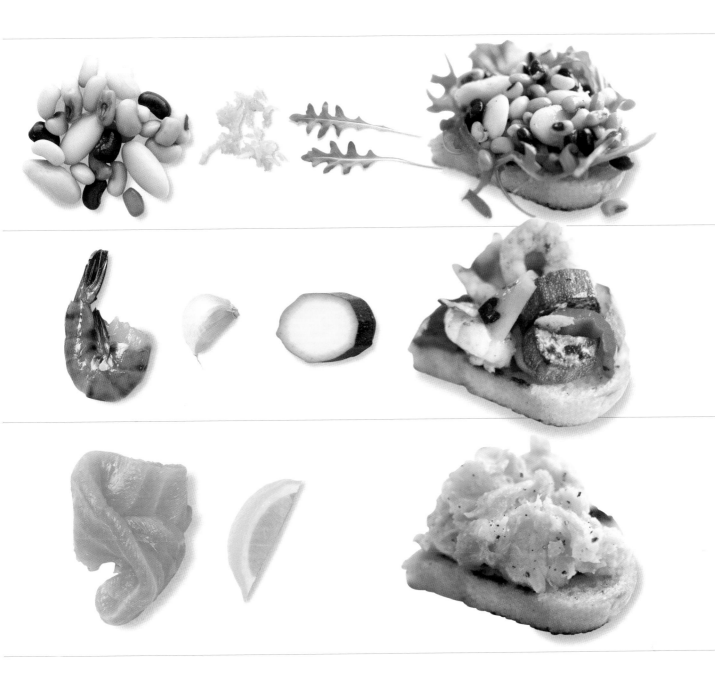

SALADS

PANZANELLA

serves 6

INGREDIENTS

5 slices country bread

100 ml (3^1/$_2$ fl oz/^{1}/$_3$ cup) extra-virgin
   olive oil

30 ml (1^1/$_2$ fl oz/^{1}/$_2$ cup) sherry vinegar
   or any other white vinegar

2 cloves garlic, crushed

pinch of sugar

salt and pepper

1 cucumber, peeled and cubed

6 plum tomatoes, deseeded and
   cubed

2 red onions, cubed

150 g (5 oz) black olives, stoned

3 bunches basil

EQUIPMENT

chopping board

knife

METHOD

Soak the bread in water for a couple of minutes and then squeeze out the excess water. Chill for up to an hour.

Place the oil, vinegar, garlic and sugar in a bowl and whisk together.

Cut the bread into chunks and place in a large bowl with the cucumber, tomatoes and onions (the vegetables and bread should all be the same size). Add the dressing and toss to coat. Season to taste.

ROCKET (ARUGULA), PARMESAN AND TOASTED PINE NUT SALAD

serves 6

INGREDIENTS

150 g (5 oz/1 cup) pine nuts

6 tbsp (1/3 cup) balsamic vinegar

200 g (7 oz) Parmesan

200 g (7 oz) wild rocket (arugula)

2 tbsp lemon juice

extra-virgin olive oil

EQUIPMENT

small frying pan

saucepan

wide peeler

METHOD

Heat the frying pan on the hob and toast the pine nuts until golden brown – they will continue to cook off the heat so watch them carefully or they will over-brown.

Place the vinegar in a pan and reduce by half or until it is syrup-like in consistency.

Shave the Parmesan with the peeler.

Place the rocket (arugula) in a bowl, add the lemon juice and drizzle over the oil. Season and toss gently with your hands.

Transfer to a plate and scatter the nuts and Parmesan over the top. Using a teaspoon, drizzle the reduced vinegar over the salad.

Variation: **BEAN AND ROCKET (ARUGULA) SALAD** serves 6 **INGREDIENTS** 150 g (5 oz) mixed cannellini and borlotti beans; extra-virgin olive oil; grated rind and juice of 2 lemons; 150 g (5 oz) wild rocket (arugula) **METHOD** Cover the beans with water in a large bowl and leave to soak overnight. Boil the beans in water for 10 minutes and then simmer for 40 minutes. Drain the beans and then drizzle with the olive oil and lemon juice and rind whilst still warm. Place the rocket (arugula) on the plate with the beans to the side – pour over any remaining oil over the rocket (arugula), season and serve, sprinkled with lemon rind.

BEEF TOMATO AND MOZZARELLA SALAD WITH BASIL DRESSING

serves 6

INGREDIENTS

2 bunches basil

iced water

6 tbsp (1/3 cup) olive oil

6 beef tomatoes

4 balls buffalo mozzarella

oil for frying

salt and pepper

EQUIPMENT

very sharp knife

chopping board

pan for frying

kitchen paper

small blender

sieve

METHOD

In a pan of boiling water blanch one bunch of basil for one minute and refresh in the iced water. Drain on kitchen paper and make sure it is completely dry – don't worry about squashing the basil. Put the basil into the blender and add the olive oil. Blend and then sieve it – you want to retain the flavoured green oil and discard the basil pulp. Core the tomatoes with the knife and slice them very thinly into rounds. Slice the mozzarella thinly too. Pick off the basil leaves from the remaining bunch. Carefully layer the tomato, basil and mozzarella together, making 6 stacks. Heat the frying oil and when it is hot fry the basil leaves. Drizzle the basil-flavoured oil over the stacks and top them with a fried basil leaf, season and serve.

PLUM TOMATO, AVOCADO AND MINT SALAD serves 6 **INGREDIENTS** juice of 2 lemons; 1 tsp Dijon mustard; pinch of sugar; salt and pepper; 4 tbsp (¼ cup) olive oil; 12 plum tomatoes, cored and quartered; 2 avocados, cut into chunks; 1 handful fresh mint leaves **METHOD** Place the lemon juice, mustard, sugar, seasoning and oil in a jam jar and shake to blend. Place the tomatoes, avocado chunks and mint in a bowl and pour the dressing over. Season and serve.

POMODORINO SALAD WITH BOCCONCINI AND CARAMELIZED RED ONIONS serves 6 **INGREDIENTS** 2 red onions, thinly sliced; 1 tbsp demerara sugar; knob of butter; 1 tbsp balsamic vinegar; 250 g (9 oz) pomodorino tomatoes, halved; 150 g (5 oz) bocconcini (mozzarella balls); 3 sprigs thyme, leaves only; extra-virgin olive oil for drizzling **METHOD** Melt the butter and cook the onions gently for at least 30 minutes, stirring every five minutes or so. You want the onions to be soft and have a good colour to them. Place the remaining ingredients in a bowl then toss the caramelized onions through, season and drizzle with olive oil.

CAPONATA serves 6 **INGREDIENTS** 1 large aubergine (eggplant), cubed; 2 courgettes (zucchini), cubed; 1 red pepper, cubed; salt and pepper; 6 tbsp (⅓ cup) olive oil; 6 asparagus spears, cut into chunks; 1 red onion, cubed; 250 g (9 oz) tinned tomatoes; 250 g (9 oz) cherry tomatoes, halved; 2 tbsp caster (superfine) sugar; 4 tbsp (¼ cup) red wine vinegar; 1 tsp ground nutmeg; 1 tbsp caper berries; 12 black olives, stoned; 1 tbsp fresh oregano **METHOD** Put the aubergine in a colander, sprinkle with ½ tsp salt and set aside for 30–60 minutes. Press gently to extract as much water as possible, then dry on kitchen paper. Heat 4 tbsp (¼ cup) olive oil in a frying pan. Sauté the asparagus until browned and set aside. Fry the aubergine in the same oil until browned and tender, adding extra oil if necessary. Leave to cool. Add the remaining oil to the pan, and sauté the onion until soft, add the tinned tomatoes and peppers and simmer for 15 minutes until thick. Add the sugar, vinegar and nutmeg, and cook gently for a further 10 minutes, until you have a rich, sweet-and-sour sauce. Stir in the courgettes, capers, olives, oregano, aubergine and asparagus. Taste and season. Serve warm.

TUNA AND BEAN SALAD

serves 6

INGREDIENTS

450 g (1 lb) fresh tuna, cut into

   chunks

250 g (9 oz) tinned butter beans

250 g (9 oz) tinned cannellini beans

grated rind and juice of 2 lemons

5 tbsp ($^1/_3$ cup) olive oil

1 small bunch flat-leaf parsley,

   leaves only

1 bunch chives, chopped

1 baby red Cos lettuce

salt and pepper

EQUIPMENT

griddle pan

METHOD

Heat the griddle pan until smoking then add the tuna and cook until marked on both sides. Do not over-cook – you want to keep the tuna rare in the middle. Set aside.

Drain the beans and rinse under running cold water. Place the beans in a bowl, add the lemon juice, oil, herbs and lettuce then the tuna.

Gently toss with your hands and put on a plate. Season and serve.

WALNUT, RADICCHIO AND GORGONZOLA SALAD

serves 6

INGREDIENTS

1 large radicchio

175 g (6 oz) Gorgonzola

50 g (2 oz) walnut halves

1 squeeze lemon

4 tbsp ($^{1}/_{4}$ cup) olive oil

salt and pepper

EQUIPMENT

knife

METHOD

Slice the radicchio into wedges. Cut or crumble the Gorgonzola and place over the radicchio. Scatter the walnuts over the top and squeeze the lemon on top, then drizzle over the oil. This salad may not need much salt but we suggest a good amount of freshly ground pepper.

ROASTED PEPPER AND GARLIC SALAD WITH ROSEMARY

serves 6

INGREDIENTS

1 whole bulb garlic

olive oil

2 red, 2 yellow and 2 green peppers,
   cut into chunky strips

2 sprigs rosemary, needles only

EQUIPMENT

griddle pan

METHOD

Pre-heat the oven to 180°C/350°F/Gas mark 4. Drizzle the garlic bulb with a little oil and place on a tray in the oven for 30 minutes. Set aside.

Heat the griddle pan until smoking and griddle the peppers until they have a good colour on both sides. When they are cooked transfer them to a bowl with the rosemary and drizzle them with oil. Carefully take the roasted cloves of garlic from the bulb and add to the bowl. Season and serve warm or cold.

MEAT AND FISH

CARPACCIO WITH PARMESAN SHAVINGS AND LAMB'S LETTUCE (CORN SALAD)

serves 6

INGREDIENTS

12 very thin slices beef fillet

1 small packet lamb's lettuce
   (corn salad)

50 g (2 oz/½ cup) Parmesan
   shavings

salt and pepper

1 lemon

extra virgin olive oil

EQUIPMENT

wide peeler

very sharp knife

pepper mill

METHOD

Lay the meat carefully on a plate, place the lamb's lettuce (corn salad) in the middle and scatter the Parmesan shavings over the top. Squeeze the lemon over the top and then drizzle over the oil. Grind some fresh black pepper on top and add a sprinkling of salt.

ANOTHER CLASSIC DRESSING INGREDIENTS 2 tbsp Worcestershire sauce; 1 tsp lemon juice; 3 tbsp mayonnaise; 2 tbsp milk; salt and pepper **METHOD** Add the Worcestershire sauce to the lemon juice and mayonnaise; add the milk just so the sauce sticks to the back of a spoon – taste and season. Add more Worcestershire sauce or lemon juice if necessary. Drizzle the dressing over the meat.

NOTE: If you can't get fresh pre-sliced beef buy a fillet steak – about 175 g (6 oz). Wrap the fillet in clingfilm and put it in the freezer for 30 minutes to chill well. With a very sharp knife slice the beef – you will have some fillet left over, which you can use in another recipe.

BRESAOLA WITH PARMESAN SHAVINGS AND WILD ROCKET (ARUGULA) serves 6 **INGREDIENTS** 12 slices bresaola; 150 g (5 oz) wild rocket (arugula); 50 g (2 oz) Parmesan shavings; walnut oil for drizzling; black pepper. **METHOD** Lay the bresaola on a plate and place the wild rocket (arugula) in the middle, scatter over the Parmesan shavings and drizzle over the walnut oil. Season and serve.

PARMA HAM WITH PARMESAN SHAVINGS AND ROCKET (ARUGULA) **INGREDIENTS** 12 slices Parma ham; 50 g (2 oz) Parmesan shavings; 150 g (5 oz) wild rocket (arugula); extra-virgin olive oil for drizzling; black pepper **METHOD** Lay the Parma ham on a plate and place the rocket (arugula) in the middle, scatter over the Parmesan shavings and drizzle over the oil. Season and serve.

TUNA CARPACCIO WITH LAMB'S LETTUCE (CORN SALAD) **INGREDIENTS** 12 thin slices yellow-fin tuna (sashimi grade); 150 g (5 oz) lamb's lettuce (corn salad); extra-virgin olive oil for drizzling; 1 lemon, cut into wedges; salt and pepper **METHOD** Lay the tuna on a plate and place the lamb's lettuce (corn salad) in the middle then drizzle over the olive oil. Season and serve. You could also serve this with ribbons of fennel and finely diced purple shallots.

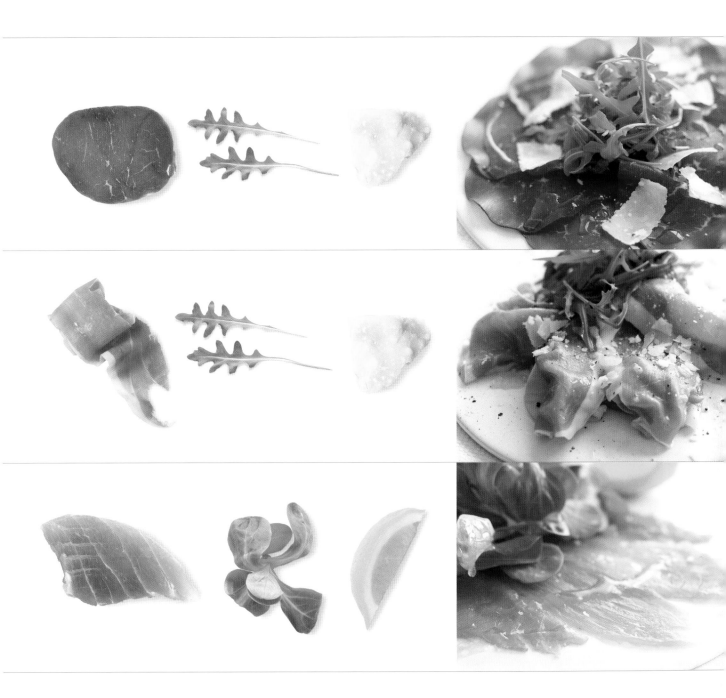

GRIDDLED ASPARAGUS WRAPPED IN SPECK

serves 6

INGREDIENTS

18 asparagus spears

9 slices Speck, cut in half lengthways

1 lemon for squeezing

olive oil for brushing and drizzling

salt and pepper

EQUIPMENT

pastry brush

griddle pan

METHOD

Heat the griddle on the hob until smoking.

Snap the hard ends of the asparagus off. Wrap the Speck around the asparagus spears, brush with a little olive oil and place on the griddle. Cook until scored on all sides. Stack on a plate.

Squeeze over the lemon, drizzle with more olive oil and season. Serve warm.

PAN-FRIED CHICKEN LIVERS WITH RED ONIONS, PEPPERS AND CRISPY SAGE

serves 6

INGREDIENTS

50 g (2 oz) butter

450 g (1 lb) chicken livers, picked over
and de-veined

2 tbsp sherry, brandy or marsala

salt and pepper

2 red onions, cut into thin wedges

2 ramiro red peppers, sliced into
circles

oil for frying

1 bunch sage, leaves only

1 lemon for squeezing

EQUIPMENT

frying pan

heavy-bottomed pan for frying

kitchen paper

kitchen tongs

METHOD

Melt half the butter in the frying pan over high heat and add the chicken livers, turning occasionally so that they get a good colour on all sides. Splash the sherry over the livers and season. Continue cooking until the liquid is reduced by half (this should take 5 minutes). Set the livers aside.

In the same pan add the red onions and the peppers and cook until soft. They want a bit of colour but not too much. Set aside.

Heat the oil in the heavy pan until just smoking, carefully add the sage leaves and cook for 30 seconds – drain on kitchen paper and set aside.

In a bowl toss all the ingredients together carefully and season well. Serve on a plate and squeeze the lemon over. Serve warm or at room temperature.

PARMESAN-COATED CHICKEN GOUJONS WITH PESTO DIP

makes 12 goujons

INGREDIENTS

PESTO DIP

1 bunch basil, leaves only

50 g (2 oz/½ cup) pine nuts

2 tbsp grated Parmesan

225 ml (8 fl oz/1 cup) extra-virgin
   olive oil

2 cloves garlic

salt and pepper

2 large chicken breasts, skinless and
   boneless

125 g (4 oz/1 cup) plain (all-purpose)
   flour, seasoned with salt and
   pepper

2 eggs, beaten

50 g (2 oz) Parmesan and
   50 g (2 oz) matzo meal, mixed
   together in a bowl

oil for frying

1 lemon for squeezing

EQUIPMENT

bowls

heavy-bottomed pan

kitchen paper

food processor

METHOD

First make the pesto. Place the basil, pine nuts, 2 tbsp of the Parmesan, olive oil, garlic and seasoning in the processor and blend until just smooth. Check the taste, season and set aside.

Cut the chicken breasts into strips – you should get about six out of each breast. Put the seasoned flour, beaten egg and the Parmesan and matzo mixture in three separate bowls. Dip the chicken strips one by one into the flour to coat all over, then place in the egg, coating all over, and finally roll them in the Parmesan and matzo mixture. Chill the coated strips in the fridge for 30 minutes.

Heat the oil until it sizzles when a crumb is put into it. Carefully fry each chicken strip – if the outside is getting rather dark take the chicken out and place in a pre-heated oven (180°C/350°F/Gas mark 4) for 5 minutes. This is to ensure that the chicken is cooked through. Once all the chicken goujons are thoroughly cooked squeeze the lemon over them and serve with the pesto on the side for dipping.

MINTED MONKFISH SPIEDINI

serves 6

INGREDIENTS

450 g (1 lb) monkfish tail, boned
   and cleaned

1 red and 1 yellow ramiro pepper

olive oil

juice of 2 lemons

1 clove garlic, crushed

1 bunch mint, leaves only

salt and pepper

1 lemon, cut into wedges

EQUIPMENT

griddle pan

skewers

pastry brush

kitchen tongs

METHOD

Heat the griddle pan on the hob until smoking.

Cut the monkfish and the peppers into bite-sized chunks. Mix the olive oil, lemon juice and garlic together. Brush the monkfish and pepper chunks with the mixture.

Lay the monkfish and peppers on the griddle in batches and cook on each side until scored. Repeat until all the chunks are cooked.

Skewer the chunks alternately with a mint leaf, monkfish, yellow pepper, mint leaf, monkfish, red pepper and so on. Season and serve with a wedge of lemon.

Variation: **SCALLOP AND SALMON BROCHETTES** serves 6 **INGREDIENTS** 125 g (4 oz) butter; 225 g (8 oz) middle cut salmon fillet, cut into chunks; 12 fresh scallops, cleaned and corals removed; salt and pepper; 1 bunch chives, finely chopped; 1 lemon for squeezing **METHOD** Melt the butter in a pan then put the pan in the fridge to allow the butter to set (about 30 minutes). Take the butter and you will see that there is a milk substance at the bottom of the pan and a layer of fat on top – discard the milk and keep the fat – this is now clarified butter. Place in a small pan and heat until the solid clarified butter is liquid again. Heat the griddle until smoking. Brush the salmon chunks and the scallops with the clarified butter and place on the griddle. Turn with tongs to get good scoring on all sides. Set aside. Add salt, pepper and chives to the remaining butter and pour over the brochettes. Squeeze with lemon and serve warm.

GARLIC MUSSELS WITH PESTO CRUST

serves 6

INGREDIENTS

225 ml (8 fl oz/1 cup) pesto
  (see page 47)

85 g (3 oz/1 cup) fresh breadcrumbs

grated rind and juice of 1 lemon

salt and pepper

12 green-lipped mussels, pre-cooked
  (frozen ones are fine)

oil for drizzling

EQUIPMENT

lemon zester

METHOD

Pre-heat the grill (broiler). Mix the pesto in with the breadcrumbs. Add a little lemon juice to the mixture, season with salt and pepper and divide it between the mussels, sprinkle with grated lemon rind and drizzle with oil. Place on a baking tray and grill (broil) until golden brown. Serve warm.

Variation: **GRILLED (BROILED) DUBLIN BAY PRAWNS (SHRIMP) WITH A LEMON AND PARSLEY CRUST**

serves 6 **INGREDIENTS** 1 small bunch flat-leaf parsley; 85 g (3 oz/1 cup) fresh breadcrumbs; grated rind and juice of 1 lemon; salt and pepper; 6 uncooked Dublin Bay prawns (langoustines), cut lengthways in half; 25 g (1 oz) butter, melted; 2 cloves garlic, crushed. **METHOD** Turn the grill (broiler) on to full. Finely chop the parsley and add to the breadcrumbs. Add the lemon juice and rind along with salt and pepper. The consistency of the mixture should be quite soft and squidgy. Divide the mixture between the prawn (shrimp) halves. Melt the butter gently with the garlic in it. Drizzle it over the prawns (shrimp) and grill (broil) until golden brown (about five minutes). Check that the prawns (shrimp) are cooked and serve immediately with a little more garlic butter poured over the top.

NOTE: If the prawns (shrimp) are not cooked and they are getting too dark in colour place in the oven for 5 minutes or until cooked through.

COURGETTE (ZUCCHINI) FLOWERS STUFFED WITH FRESH ANCHOVIES AND MOZZARELLA

serves 6

INGREDIENTS

100 g (3¹/₂ oz/1 cup) plain (all-purpose) flour

2 tbsp olive oil

5 tbsp (¹/₃ cup) dry white wine

1 egg, separated

salt and pepper

150 ml (5 fl oz/¹/₂ cup) warm water

6 courgette (zucchini) flowers, with the baby courgettes (zucchini) attached

150 g (5 oz) mozzarella, cut into 12 small rectangles

6 white anchovies

6 large basil leaves

oil for deep-frying

EQUIPMENT

electric whisk

heavy-bottomed pan

kitchen paper

metal bowl

METHOD

Mix together the flour, oil, wine and egg yolk in a bowl and season with salt and pepper. Slowly add the warm water, whisking all the time until you have a batter that coats the back of a spoon. Leave to stand for 30 minutes.

Carefully prize open the courgette (zucchini) flowers, trying not to rip the petals too much. Take a piece of mozzarella and wrap the anchovy and then the basil leaf around it. Stuff it into the centre of the flower and then twist the tips of the petals together to enclose the stuffing. Repeat until all the flowers are stuffed.

Heat the oil for frying. In a metal bowl whisk up the whites and fold into the batter. Dip the flowers, with the courgettes (zucchini), into the batter and fry in the hot oil until crispy and golden brown. Drain on the kitchen paper and serve immediately.

COURGETTE (ZUCCHINI) FLOWERS STUFFED WITH PRAWNS (SHRIMP)

serves 6 **INGREDIENTS** 100 g (3^1/$_2$ oz) plain (all-purpose) flour; 2 tbsp olive oil; 5 tbsp dry white wine; 1 egg, separated; salt and pepper; 150 ml (5 fl oz) warm water; 6 courgette (zucchini) flowers, with courgettes attached; 200 g (7 oz) peeled cooked prawns (shrimp); 100 g (3^1/$_2$ oz) robiola cheese, cut into cubes; grated rind of 1 lemon; 3 stems thyme, leaves only; oil for frying **METHOD** Mix together the flour, oil, wine and egg yolk in a bowl and season. Slowly add the warm water, whisking all the time until you have a batter that coats the back of a spoon. Leave to stand for 30 minutes. Carefully open the courgette flowers, trying not to rip the petals. Mix together the prawns, cheese, lemon rind and thyme, salt and pepper and carefully stuff a little of the mixture into the centre of each flower. Twist the tips of the petals together to enclose the stuffing. Repeat with all the flowers. Heat the oil for frying. In a metal bowl whisk up the whites and fold into the batter. Dip the flowers into the batter and fry as before (see page 53). Serve immediately.

COURGETTE (ZUCCHINI) FLOWERS STUFFED WITH OLIVE AND GARLIC CREAM CHEESE

INGREDIENTS 100 g (3^1/$_2$ oz/1 cup) plain (all-purpose) flour; 2 tbsp olive oil; 5 tbsp dry white wine; 1 egg, separated; salt and pepper; 150 ml (5 fl oz) warm water; 6 courgette (zucchini) flowers, with courgettes attached; 200 g (4 oz) black olives, stoned and roughly chopped; 100 g (3^1/$_2$ oz) cream cheese; 3 cloves garlic, crushed; oil for frying **METHOD** Make the batter (see above) and leave to stand for 30 minutes. Carefully open the courgette flowers, trying not to rip the petals . Mix the olives, cream cheese and garlic together, season and carefully stuff a little of the mixture into the centre of each flower and then twist the tips of the petals together to enclose the stuffing. Repeat with all the flowers. Heat the oil for frying. In a metal bowl whisk up the whites and fold into the batter. Dip the flowers into the batter and fry as before (see page 53). Serve immediately.

COURGETTE (ZUCCHINI) FLOWERS STUFFED WITH GRATED COURGETTES (ZUCCHINI) AND HERBS

INGREDIENTS 100 g (3^1/$_2$ oz/1 cup) plain (all-purpose) flour; 2 tbsp olive oil; 5 tbsp dry white wine; 1 egg, separated; salt and pepper; 150 ml (5 fl oz) warm water; 6 courgette (zucchini) flowers, with the courgettes attached; 200 g (7 oz) grated courgettes (zucchini); 1 tbsp each of chopped basil, flat-leaf parsley, sage; 3 stems thyme, leaves only; oil for frying **METHOD** Make the batter (see above) and leave to stand for 30 minutes. Carefully open the courgette flowers, trying not to rip the petals . Mix the grated courgettes and herbs together, season with salt and pepper and carefully stuff a little of the mixture into the centre of each flower and then twist the tips of the petals together to enclose the stuffing. Repeat with all the flowers. Heat the oil for frying. In a metal bowl whisk up the whites and fold into the batter. Dip the flowers into the batter and fry as before (see page 53). Serve immediately.

FRITTO MISTO DI MARE

serves 6

INGREDIENTS

12 cuttlefish, cleaned and ready
    to cook

1 bunch basil

iced water

225 ml (8 fl oz/1 cup) extra-virgin
    olive oil

125 g (4 oz/1 cup) plain (all-purpose)
    flour

salt and pepper

12 raw tiger prawns (shrimp), peeled
    but with the tails on

oil for frying

coarse sea salt and freshly ground
    black pepper

1 lemon for squeezing

EQUIPMENT

saucepan

blender

sieve

bowl

heavy-bottomed frying pan

kitchen paper

METHOD

Ask your fishmonger to clean and prepare the cuttlefish for you.

In a pan of boiling water blanch the basil for one minute and refresh in the iced water. Drain on kitchen paper and make sure it is completely dry – don't worry about squashing the basil. Put it into the blender and add the olive oil. Blend and then sieve it – you want to retain the green oil and discard the basil pulp. Place in a dipping bowl.

Place the flour in a bowl and season it. Dip the prawns (shrimp) and cuttlefish in the flour so it is coated and pat until no flour comes off.

Heat the oil for frying and fry the fish until golden brown. Drain on kitchen paper and sprinkle with salt. Serve warm, with the basil oil and squeezed lemon drizzled over.

SOUPS

TUSCAN BEAN SOUP

serves 6

INGREDIENTS

400 g (14 oz/2 cups) dried Tuscan
  beans (cannellini and borlotti)

125 ml (4 fl oz/¹/₂ cup) olive oil

2 cloves garlic, finely chopped

1 onion, diced

1 stick celery, diced

2 sprigs rosemary, needles only,
  finely chopped

3 rashers streaky bacon, diced

5 tsp tomato purée (paste) or
  420 g (14 oz) tinned peeled
  tomatoes

2 leeks, diced

2 courgettes (zucchini), diced

1 bunch basil

2 sprigs parsley

salt and pepper

EQUIPMENT

blender

large saucepan

METHOD

Soak the beans overnight in water. Drain and gently cook the beans in fresh water for about 2 hours, or until tender. Drain, reserving the liquid, and put about half the beans through a fine sieve or blender. Set aside.

Heat the oil in a large pan and gently sauté the garlic, onion, celery, rosemary and bacon until they begin to brown. Mix the tomato purée (paste) with a dash of warm water and stir into pan. Add the, leeks, courgettes (zucchini), basil and parsley, as well as the puréed and whole beans, and their cooking water. Add a little extra hot water if necessary. This should be a thick soup so don't add too much. Season and taste, then cook for a further 30 minutes. Serve hot.

Variation: **WHITE BEAN SOUP** serves 6 **INGREDIENTS** 2 cloves garlic, crushed ; 2 large banana shallots; 3 rashers smoked bacon, finely diced; 1 tbsp tomato purée (paste); 600 ml (1 pint) strong chicken stock (or 2 chicken stock cubes, diluted); 1 tin butter beans; 1 tin cannellini beans; 125 ml (4 fl oz) sherry; salt and pepper; 1 tbsp olive oil; 1 small sprig flat-leaf parsley **METHOD** Fry the garlic, shallots and bacon in a pan until golden brown. Add the tomato purée and chicken stock along with the beans and sherry. Simmer for 1 hour. Season, add the oil and more water if the soup is too thick. Garnish with parsley.

TOMATO AND BASIL SOUP

Serves 6

INGREDIENTS

1 onion, diced

25 g (1 oz) butter

1 tbsp olive oil

1.3 kg (3 lb) plum tomatoes, roughly
chopped

2 cloves garlic, chopped

700 ml ($1^1/_4$ pt/$2^1/_2$ cups) strong
chicken stock

125 ml (4 fl oz/$^1/_2$ cup) white wine

2 tbsp tomato purée (paste)

1 bunch basil

METHOD

Cook the onion in the butter and oil until soft. Add the tomatoes and garlic. Cook for 15 minutes until softened then add the stock, wine and tomato purée (paste). Simmer for a further 30 minutes, stirring occasionally. You want the soup to be thick and a rich red colour. Blend the soup with half of the basil then pass it through a sieve to catch the seeds and skin of the tomatoes. Return the soup to the heat, taste, season and serve, garnished with the remaining basil.

TOMATO AND BREAD SOUP serves 6 **INGREDIENTS** 1 onion, diced; 25 g (1 oz) butter; 1 tbsp olive oil; 1.3 kg (3 lb) plum tomatoes, roughly chopped; 2 cloves garlic, chopped; 700 ml (1¼ pt/2½ cups) strong chicken stock; 125 ml (4 fl oz/ ½ cup) white wine; 2 tbsp tomato purée (paste); 1 small bunch basil; 4 slices country bread; 1 clove garlic **METHOD** Cook the onion in the butter and oil until soft. Add the tomatoes and garlic. Cook for 15 minutes until softened then add the stock, wine and tomato purée (paste). Simmer for a further 30 minutes, stirring occasionally. You want the soup to be thick and a rich red colour. Blend the soup with half of the basil then pass it through a sieve to catch the seeds and skin of the tomatoes. Rub the slices of bread with the clove of garlic and then cut the slices into cubes. Add them to the soup. Return the soup to the heat, taste, season and serve, garnished with the remaining basil.

TOMATO, BEAN AND THYME SOUP serves 6 **INGREDIENTS** 1 onion, diced; 25 g (1 oz) butter; 1 tbsp olive oil; 1.3 kg (3 lb) plum tomatoes, roughly chopped; 2 cloves garlic, chopped; 700 ml (1¼ pt/2½ cups) strong chicken stock; 125 ml (4 fl oz/¼ cup) white wine; 2 tbsp tomato purée (paste); 3 sprigs thyme, leaves only; 1 x 400-g (14-oz) tin mixed beans; olive oil for drizzling **METHOD** Cook the onion in the butter and oil until soft. Add the tomatoes and garlic. Cook for 15 minutes until softened then add the stock, wine and tomato purée (paste). Simmer for a further 30 minutes, stirring occasionally. The soup should be a rich red colour. Blend the soup then pass it through a sieve to catch the seeds and skin of the tomatoes. Return the soup to the heat, add the beans, thyme (reserve a little for garnish) and oil and cook for a further 15 minutes. If the soup is getting too thick, add some hot water. Taste, season and serve, garnish with fresh thyme and drizzled with olive oil.

CHILLED TOMATO SOUP WITH BASIL OIL serves 6 **INGREDIENTS** oil for frying; 5 cloves garlic, chopped; 2 slices county bread, diced; 1 onion, diced; 25 g (1 oz) butter; 1 tbsp olive oil; 1.3 kg (3 lb) plum tomatoes, roughly chopped; 700 ml (1¼ pt/2½ cups) strong chicken stock; 125 ml (4 fl oz/½ cup) white wine; 2 tbsp tomato purée (paste); 225 g (8 oz) mascarpone plus extra to garnish; basil oil to drizzle (see page 29); **METHOD** Heat the oil for frying and add half the garlic. When it is crispy add the diced bread. Drain the croûtons and set aside, discarding the garlic. Cook the onion in the butter and oil until soft. Add the tomatoes and remaining garlic. Cook for 15 minutes until softened then add the stock, wine and tomato purée. Simmer for 30 minutes, stirring occasionally. Blend the soup with half of the basil then pass through a sieve. Fold in the mascarpone. Ladle into soup bowls and garnish with more mascarpone, a drizzle of basil oil and a few croûtons.

MINESTRONE ALLA GENOVESE

serves 6

INGREDIENTS

3 tbsp olive oil

1 onion, diced

2 celery sticks, thinly sliced

1.2 L (2 pt/4 cups) strong vegetable
   stock

salt and pepper

3 tablespoons tomato purée (paste)

150 g (5 oz) French beans

1 courgette (zucchini), thinly sliced

1 potato, diced

1/2 Savoy cabbage, shredded

1 aubergine (eggplant), diced

6 fresh plum tomatoes, peeled and
   de-seeded, chopped

125 g (4 oz) short pasta, e.g.
   macaroni

225 ml (8 fl oz) pesto (see page 47)

EQUIPMENT

large saucepan

large frying pan or wok

METHOD

Gently fry the onion and celery in the oil. Add the stock, seasoning and tomato purée (paste) and bring to the boil.

In a large frying pan flash-fry the courgette (zucchini), potato, cabbage, aubergine (eggplant), French beans and tomatoes just enough to get a bit of colour on them. Add them to the stock and reduce the heat for about 30 minutes.

Add the pasta to the soup and simmer for a further 10 minutes, or until the pasta is cooked.

Ladle the soup into bowls and top each serving with a generous spoonful of pesto.

SWEET RED PEPPER AND OREGANO SOUP

serves 6

INGREDIENTS

2 onions, diced

50 g (2 oz) butter

2 x 325-g (11-oz) jars cooked red
peppers, drained

1 x 250-g tin (8-oz) chopped tomatoes

1 tbsp demerara sugar

600 ml (1 pt/2 cups) strong chicken
stock

1 tbsp Dijon mustard

salt and pepper

3 sprigs oregano, leaves only

EQUIPMENT

blender

METHOD

Cook the onions in the butter very gently for at least 15 minutes – you want to cook them until they are very soft and sweet, almost caramelized. Add the red peppers, tinned tomatoes, sugar, stock and mustard. Simmer gently for 30 minutes. Place the soup in the blender with the oregano (reserve some for garnish) and blend until smooth. Season and taste. Serve garnished with oregano.

SPINACH AND NUTMEG SOUP

serves 6

INGREDIENTS

1 L (1³/₄ pt/3¹/₂ cups) chicken stock

40 g (1¹/₂ oz) butter

2 onions, finely chopped

40 g (1¹/₂ oz/¹/₂ cup) plain

   (all-purpose) flour

500 g (1 lb 2 oz) frozen spinach,

   defrosted

juice of 2 lemons

300 ml (10 fl oz/1¹/₄ cups) double

   (heavy) cream, whipped

salt and pepper

fresh nutmeg

EQUIPMENT

blender

nutmeg grater

METHOD

Heat the stock until boiling. Melt the butter in a pan and add the onions, gently cooking until soft. Stir in the flour to make a roux. Add the hot stock little by little, continuing to stir the roux, add the spinach and lemon juice and cook for about 10 minutes.

Blend the soup until nearly smooth. Pour back into the pan and add the cream (reserving a little for the garnish), nutmeg and seasoning. Serve immediately with a garnish of whipped cream and grated nutmeg.

NIBBLES

PARMESAN CRISPS

serves 6

INGREDIENTS

250 g (9 oz/1 cup) grated Parmesan

EQUIPMENT

7.5-cm (3-in) cutter

tablespoon

greaseproof paper

baking sheet

rolling pin (optional)

METHOD

Pre-heat the oven to 200°C/400°F/Gas mark 6. Line the baking sheet with greaseproof paper. Place the cutter on the tray and drop in a level tablespoon of Parmesan, take the cutter away and slightly flatten down the Parmesan so it makes a circle – there should be enough Parmesan to cover the whole circle. Repeat this until all the Parmesan is used up.

Place in the oven for 5 minutes, or until the Parmesan starts to bubble and turn a golden yellow. You need to watch them carefully, as the Parmesan burns very quickly.

Take the baking sheet out of the oven and let the crisps rest for a minute then, using a fish slice, lift them out carefully. If you prefer curly crisps, get a rolling pin and carefully mould the crisps over it.

Variation: **PARMESAN CRISPS WITH FENNEL SEEDS** serves 6 **INGREDIENTS** 250 g (9 oz/1 cup) grated Parmesan; 3 tbsp fennel seeds **METHOD** Pre-heat the oven to 200°C/400°F/Gas mark 6. Place the cutter on the tray and drop in a level tablespoon of Parmesan, take the cutter away and slightly flatten down the Parmesan so it makes a circle – there should be enough Parmesan to cover the whole circle. Repeat this until all the Parmesan is used up. Sprinkle with fennel seeds. Place in the oven for 5 minutes, or until the Parmesan starts to bubble and turn a golden yellow. You need to watch them carefully, as the Parmesan burns very quickly. Take the baking sheet out of the oven and let the crisps rest for a minute then, using a fish slice, lift them out carefully. If you prefer curly crisps, get a rolling pin and carefully mould the crisps over it.

CRISPY OLIVES

serves 6

INGREDIENTS

oil for frying

350 g (12 oz) stoned stuffed olives

1 egg, beaten with a dash of milk

125 g (4 oz/1 cup) plain (all-purpose) flour

85 g (3 oz/1¹/₂ cups) Japanese breadcrumbs

EQUIPMENT

heavy-bottomed pan

kitchen paper

METHOD

Heat the oil for frying in a large heavy-bottomed pan. Drain the olives and pat them dry, roll them in the flour so they are coated then drop them into the egg and cover them completely. Finally roll them in the Japanese breadcrumbs. When the oil is hot place the olives in the pan and cook until the crumbs are golden brown. Serve warm.

Variations: **SPICY OLIVES** serves 6 **INGREDIENTS** 350 g (12 oz) large olives, stoned; olive oil for drizzling; 2 red snub-nose chillies, very finely diced **METHOD** Drain the olives and sprinkle with the diced chilli. Be careful – don't rub your eyes after handling chillies! Drizzle with olive oil and serve.

HERBED OLIVES serves 6 **INGREDIENTS** 350 g (12 oz) large olives, stoned; olive oil for drizzling; 2 tbsp fresh mixed chopped herbs (tarragon, parsley, oregano, basil, thyme) **METHOD** Drain the olives and roll them in the mixed herbs. Drizzle with oil and serve.

CITRUS OLIVES serves 6 **INGREDIENTS** 350 g (12 oz) large olives, stoned; olive oil for drizzling; grated rind of 3 lemons **METHOD** Drain the olives and sprinkle them with the lemon rind. Drizzle oil over them and serve.

TOMATO FRITTERS

Serves 6

INGREDIENTS

SAVOURY CHOUX PASTRY

125 ml (4 fl oz/$1/2$ cup) water

50 g (2 oz) unsalted butter

salt and pepper

75 g ($2^3/4$ oz/$3/4$ cup) plain
   (all-purpose) flour

2 eggs

100 g (4 oz/1 cup) grated Parmesan

18 cherry tomatoes or baby plum
   tomatoes

100 g ($3^1/2$ oz) mozzarella, chopped
   into small cubes

1 small bunch basil, leaves torn
   into small pieces

2 fresh white anchovy fillets, finely
   chopped

salt and pepper

vegetable oil for frying

EQUIPMENT

saucepan

wooden spoon

heavy-bottomed pan

kitchen roll

METHOD

First make the choux pastry. Pour the water into a saucepan. Add the butter, salt and pepper and bring the mixture to the boil. Take the pan off the heat and gently tip in all the flour all in one go. Stirring constantly, heat again and cook until the mixture turns into a smooth, glossy paste and comes away from the side of the pan. Take the pan off the heat and leave to cool. Beat the eggs into the mixture one at a time. Stir in the grated Parmesan at the end.

Slice off the top of the tomatoes (the end where the stalk is), scoop out the pulp and place upside down to drain out any juice.

In a bowl mix the mozzarella, basil and anchovies together then season with salt and pepper. Fill the tomatoes with the cheese mixture.

Take a small amount of the choux mixture (about the size of a ping pong ball) and make a flat pattie in your hand. Place the tomato in the middle and wrap the choux mixture around it so the tomato is totally covered. Roll it in your hand. Heat the oil until slightly smoking. Drop the fritters into the hot oil until they puff up and go golden brown. Take out of the oil with a slotted spoon and drain on kitchen paper.

Serve immediately, garnished with fresh basil.

BAGNA CAUDA WITH FRESH VEGETABLES

serves 6

INGREDIENTS

225 ml (8 fl oz/1 cup) extra-virgin
   olive oil

6 fresh white anchovy fillets

6 sprigs flat-leaf parsley, leaves only

juice of 2 lemons

salt and pepper

1 bunch baby asparagus

1 bunch baby purple spring onions
   (scallions)

1 head baby celery

1 bunch baby carrots

1 punnet mixed red and yellow cherry
   tomatoes

EQUIPMENT

blender

METHOD

Place the oil, anchovy fillets, parsley and lemon juice in a food processor or blender and whizz until you have a coarsely
blended dip.

Wash and trim the vegetables, if necessary and arrange on a platter. Gently heat the dip, if liked, and place in a bowl
surrounded by the fresh vegetables.

INDEX